This book is dedicated to Zakk, Blake, and Ava, who are such a very big part of our lives.

Upcoming books in the Soul Kids Series

- *Being an Empath Kid*
- *Being a Crystal Kid*
- *Being in a Step Family*
- *Being Safe and Protected*

There is only one you

Draw a picture of yourself

Your name: _____

You were created perfectly, just like everyone else in the world.

All of the wonderful things about you on the outside are just a very small part of who you are.

On the inside you have so many amazing things about you and these are the things that matter most!

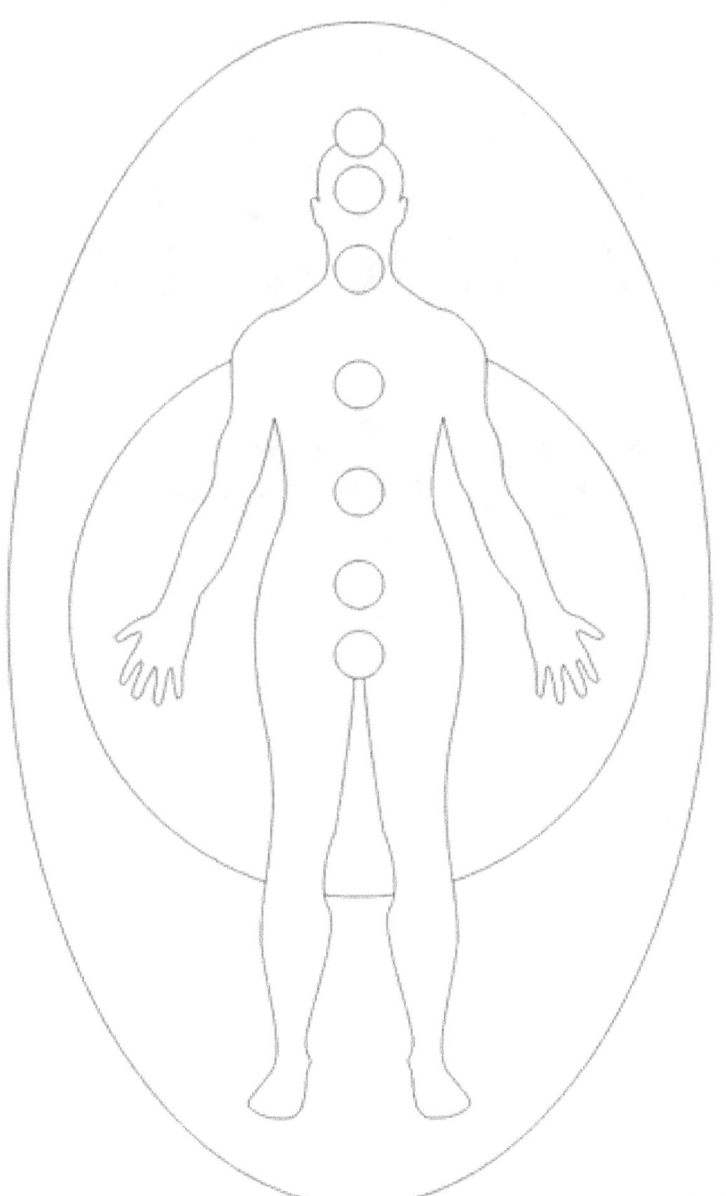

Crown Chakra

is WHITE

Third Eye Chakra

is INDIGO

Throat Chakra

Is BLUE

Heart Chakra

is GREEN

Solar Plexus Chakra

is YELLOW

Sacral Chakra

is ORANGE

Base Chakra

Is RED

These could be things like...

Your mind and how you think.

Sad

Confused

Angry

Energetic

Appreciated

Lonely Shy Excited

Loved

Your emotions and what you feel.

Your dreams and what you love.

Your skills and the way you learn best.

What you believe in.

Who you love
and care about.

But the most important thing is to remember how you feel about YOURSELF.

This is more important than how other people feel about you or see you.

What are some of the things that YOU feel about yourself?

What makes you, YOU?

You can draw, paint, write or have a grown up write your thoughts for you.

How do you feel right now?

All feelings are important, and we all feel them at certain times. It's OK to feel angry, sad, excited, scared, happy or nervous, or any of the many other feelings you may feel.

What are your dreams?

It is always important to follow your dreams and goals, and remember that you can do anything if you try.

What do you believe in?

You can believe what you want to believe. It does not matter what other people say or think about your beliefs, because they are yours and yours alone.

Who do you love and care about?

There may be many people and animals in your life that you love and care about. Remember to always love and care about yourself.

What do you like to do?

There may be lots of things that you like to do. These might not always be the same things that your friends like and that's okay.

How do you feel about yourself?

The most important thing is how you feel about yourself. There are lots of amazing things about you that make you special.

There is only one you, so be who you are!

www.ingramcontent.com/pod-product-compliance
Lightning Source LLC
Chambersburg PA
CBHW060531010526
44110CB00052B/2569